IMAGES
of America

NEW JERSEY
COAST GUARD STATIONS
AND RUMRUNNERS

IMAGES
of America

NEW JERSEY
COAST GUARD STATIONS
AND RUMRUNNERS

Van R. Field and John J. Galluzzo

ARCADIA

First published 2004

Published by Arcadia Publishing,
Charleston SC, Chicago IL, Portsmouth NH, San Francisco CA

Printed in Great Britain

Library of Congress Catalog Card Number: 2004102492

For all general information, contact Arcadia Publishing:
Telephone 843-853-2070
Fax 843-853-0044
E-mail sales@arcadiapublishing.com
For customer service and orders:
Toll-free 1-888-313-2665

Visit us on the Internet at www.arcadiapublishing.com

This book can only be dedicated to one group of people: those men and women who have worked on the New Jersey shore as volunteers or in service with the U.S. Life-Saving Service and with the Coast Guard, risking their own lives so that others might live and standing Semper Paratus, always prepared, when the call comes out.

CONTENTS

INTRODUCTION

The New Jersey of Capt. Eugene Topping Osborn's time was not the New Jersey of today, and the U.S. Coast Guard of Osborn's time was not the Coast Guard of today. In both cases, though, their spirits survive in the structures and the people of today's Coast Guard.

During Osborn's time in the service of his country—from 1913 to 1946—the Coast Guard underwent significant and even drastic changes. In 1913, there was no Coast Guard as we know it now, at least not in one recognizable body. Osborn started out as a surfman in the last years of the U.S. Life-Saving Service, a national organization that boasted more than 275 stations at its height in 1914, but which had its meager beginning in small shacks along the New Jersey shore in the late 1840s. In 1915, under pressure to fall under Pres. William Howard Taft's political watchword "unifunctionalism," meaning one department with one function, the Life-Saving Service merged with the Revenue Cutter Service under the Department of the Treasury to form the U.S. Coast Guard.

In 1915, the shoreside stations of the Coast Guard, the subject of Osborn's camera lens and therefore of this book, came in various forms—from ornate, high-Victorian styles to simple Red House, one-floor structures to regionally specific styles like the Jersey pattern. Crews consisted of men who until that time had been considered civilians but were now thrown into the spit-and-polish world of the military, a consequence of their new association with the sailing men of the Revenue Cutter Service.

Much of the routine drilling of the old days carried over into the new service, and for a while the equipment remained the same. The line-throwing gun and breeches buoy still saved lives, and the pulling lifeboats and surf boats of rugged fame still made their weekly appearances for capsize drills all around the United States. Motorized lifeboats, though, had crept into wider and wider use as the first decade of the 20th century ended, and they would eventually force their manually powered competitors into retirement, much to the delight of both the weary-armed crewmen and shipwreck victims waiting for help to arrive.

With almost no time to get acclimated to its new form, the Coast Guard entered World War I under the direction of the U.S. Navy, as mandated by presidential orders. Men who had once patrolled beaches as surfmen looking for shipwrecks now watched the same shorelines for German U-boats. Those with shipboard experience found themselves on escorts crossing the Atlantic, helping keep America's shipping interests alive and, later, transporting fighting men to the great battlefields of Europe.

Almost as quickly as the war ended, the Coast Guard embarked on a new one. With the passage of the Volstead Act in 1920, the federal government had the law-enforcement tool it needed to wage war on the illegal smuggling of illicit booze, as the grand and noble experiment of national alcohol prohibition became the law of the land. The Coast Guard soon became the number one crime-stopping agency along the coast with the discovery of the formation off the Jersey Shore of Rum Row, a line of ships waiting just beyond the boundaries of international waters with decks and holds loaded with pure, distilled, or watered-down liquor from Bermuda,

France, and other ports, available for men and women daring enough to run the gauntlet to shore. High-speed chases led to the confiscation of boats and cargo, to unfortunate deaths of both rumrunners and coastguardsmen, and to the uncharted waters of a public relations nightmare for a service used to being adored. Always known as the "storm warriors," who charged into the pounding surf to save lives when all others turned and fled to higher ground, and beloved as heroes in popular newspapers and magazines of the day, the Coast Guard had now become the hated law enforcement agency stopping Americans from having their fun with a little drink here and there. For 14 long years, the Coast Guard bore the brunt of this unfair assault by the American people, until Prohibition's ultimate repeal in 1933. Tested by public scrutiny and faced with new challenges, the Coast Guard survived and grew, absorbing the Bureau of Navigation, the Steamboat Inspection Service, and the U.S. Lighthouse Establishment.

The job of overseeing the shoreside stations of New Jersey during the 1920s and 1930s put Osborn in contact with the men of all 41 stations from Sandy Hook to Cape May during that time period. The photograph collection he amassed captured the waning days of the active Life-Saving Service stations before their phasing out and abandonment or destruction in the face of new construction or relocation. Because of advancements in radio and motor lifeboat technology, the Coast Guard no longer needed the vigilance of surfmen patrolling every inch of beach of New Jersey's barrier islands on foot. Stations grew farther and farther apart and lesser in number as the years passed. Many survived through World War II, as the Coast Guard sons of the old Life-Saving Service surfmen walked the same beaches to watch for the same enemy their fathers had in World War I. But after the war, many more closed for good.

Osborn's collection of photographs captured the structures, people, and events of the late 1920s and early 1930s along the New Jersey shore as they pertained to the service for which he worked. Osborn did not gather every name nor write down the details of every story, but in some instances, a picture needs very few words in support of the message it clearly passes on. Every station in the state is represented in this book by at least one photograph, and many by more than one. The hardworking coastguardsmen of the era stare back at us today with the confidence they held then, both during the Roaring Twenties, when life was good, and the Great Depression, when they were just happy to have jobs. Bags, sacks, and barrels of booze fill pages as reminders of America's second-greatest self-test (the Civil War being the first), and captured boats, pressed into service against their former employers, invoke tales of chases on the high seas, which sometimes ended in disaster.

These men, both coastguardsmen and rumrunners, waged a war that lasted far too long, leaving a tarnished image on a dignified service that did not easily wash away. Osborn's camera captured in an amazing way this time capsule of life on the New Jersey shore in a time that has now long since passed.

One

SANDY HOOK
TO SQUAN BEACH

Because of its role as guardian of the southern approach to the Hudson River, Sandy Hook Lifesaving Station was one of the first built in the United States, in 1848. Various other buildings followed the first small boathouse that originally stood watch over the waters, such as this Bibb No. 2–type structure, constructed from 1890 to 1891 and still in use in the 1930s. The station (in the abstract sense, not this specific structure) has been relocated several times through the years for one reason or another, but that has never stopped the Coast Guard from doing its duty. In fact, the station has had true heroes in its past: keeper John C. Patterson earned a Gold Life-Saving Medal, and surfmen John Redmond, John H. Pearce, John H. Smith, David Kittell, Henry A. Bennett, and Edward Brand received Silver Life-Saving Medals for their actions in rescuing the crew from the yacht *Foam* during a heavy onshore gale on July 27, 1885.

In 1938, the Work Relief and Public Works Appropriation Act provided needed funds for a boathouse, launch way, and bulkheading, as well as new boats and equipment. With the aid of winches, the marine railways (seen clearly on the right) helped bring the heavy motor lifeboats into the stations after deployment. It was a time when the necessities of lifeboat design had finally outraced human strength.

A large crew at the Sandy Hook Coast Guard Station has turned out to be photographed for Captain Osborn's album. Unfortunately, the captain did not record every name of every coastguardsman.

The first lifesaving station at Spermaceti Cove, two and a half miles south of the Sandy Hook Lighthouse, stood in good condition in 1930. Replaced by a Red House–type structure in 1872, it ran into trouble in the 1890s because it stood within range of the United States Army's Ordnance Department proving grounds.

The original building was still in such good condition that the Coast Guard decided to celebrate its historic past by rededicating it on May 21, 1930, as seen in this photograph. The building, which is the oldest federal lifesaving station in the United States, still stands today at Twin Lights National Historic Site.

In 1894, because the Red House–type station had become outdated, the Life-Saving Service constructed a Duluth-type building at Spermaceti Cove, far from the guns of the U.S. Army and with a tall watchtower from which the surfmen could watch for ships in peril. The station stayed in service into the 1930s.

Today, the Duluth-type station of the crew of Spermaceti Cove, pictured here, is maintained as a museum by the Gateway National Recreation Area at Sandy Hook.

Seabright Station, a Bibb No. 2–type structure like Sandy Hook, stood about a mile south of the Navesink Lighthouse. This image is unusual in that the early 1876 station that preceded the Bibb No. 2 still stands alongside the newer structure. Oftentimes, the service destroyed outdated buildings to make way for newer stations. The surfmen at Seabright had an advantage: a railroad track running in front of the station. In times of danger, when calls came from distant parts of the station's area of operation, or when they were called upon to aid neighboring stations, the lifesavers had the opportunity to call on railroad conductors to convey them to the scene of a rescue, equipment and all. The energy saved by not manually dragging a lifeboat to a wreck could be applied later, when bent over an oar or hauling on a breeches buoy line.

The original Monmouth Beach Station was built in 1849, the second federal lifesaving station constructed. It was eventually replaced in 1872 by a Red House–type structure. After a horrific storm on April 11 and 12, 1894, which threatened to destroy the station, the Life-Saving Service sought another plot of land nearby and constructed this Duluth-type structure in 1895.

Close examination of the watchtower reveals an unusual outdoor crow's nest, a modification from the standard Duluth-type structure seen elsewhere in New Jersey and around the United States. Today, this station is being preserved.

A large complement of coastguardsmen served at Monmouth Beach during the Prohibition era, as evidenced by this crew photograph.

A smaller crew operated out of Long Branch Station, originally built at Green Pond but later moved, according to the *1882 Annual Report* of the Life-Saving Service, because "the march of town improvements made it necessary."

Also the site of an original 1849 station, Asbury Park later sported perhaps the most ornate and decorative lifesaving station in the country, the Deal Life-Saving Station. As the style originated here, with architect Paul Pelz's design, the classification bears the name Deal type. Three other stations were built along these lines. The crews at Deal saved lives no matter what type of building they worked out of. In May 1882, before the completion of this structure, the Deal crews rescued 61 people from the sinking *Pliny*; 10 years later, in March 1892, they rescued 48 people from the *Wyndermere*. It did not matter how fancy the station was, as long as the people working inside were courageous enough to do their jobs when the call went out for help.

The Deal crew in 1930 consisted of the following men, pictured here from left to right: (first row) William Midgett, William Butler, F. Wheaton, and unidentified; (second row) C. Midgett, E. Midgett, Lee Daisy, and unidentified. The Midgett family is among the Coast Guard's most famous, historic, and accomplished lifesaving families.

Down the coast at the Shark River Station, crew members were, from left to right, as follows: (first row) ? Newman, F. Bailey, and two unidentified men; (second row) ? Pickett, C. D. Murphy, two unidentified men, and Allen Moore.

Life-Saving Service historian Ralph Shanks, coauthor of *The United States Life-Saving Service: Heroes, Rescues and Architecture of the Early Coast Guard*, once asked a retired coastguardsman how many people he thought a lifeboat could hold. In true gritty old-time Coast Guard style, the gentleman answered that he had never found out. There was always room for one more person on *his* lifeboat. It looks, though, like the crew at Shark River tried to find the real answer one day. The boat is so full, obviously for a pleasure trip with the locals or family and friends, that it is even hard to find the crew members themselves. At least we can hope that the burly man at the tiller knew what he was doing.

The fourth station at Spring Lake, listed as the Wreck Pond Lifesaving Station until 1883, became a Quonochontaug-type structure in 1895. The style derived its name from the home of the original design in Quonochontaug, Rhode Island. The structure served the Coast Guard off and on for the early decades of the 20th century.

The station was discontinued in 1917 and served as an auxiliary unit to Manasquan (also called Squan Beach) Station for several years. The unit became active again in 1925, yet was discontinued once more in 1934.

Located at Point Pleasant, the Duluth-type Manasquan (or Squan Beach) Lifesaving Station was built in 1902 and still stands today on the site of an 1856 station. In June 1903, keeper Robert F. Longstreet, Capt. John K. Andersen, and Charles H. Boker earned Gold Life-Saving Medals and Harry Andersen earned a Silver Life-Saving Medal for their heroic conduct while rescuing local fishermen from a capsized boat. The heavily laden fishing boat under the command of Captain Anderson, with Harry Anderson and five others aboard, flipped in the surf, tossing all clear. All managed to make it back to the overturned boat, though, as Boker, a fisherman watching from shore, implored others to join him in going to their aid in a skiff. Captain Longstreet, without a crew during the summer off-season, arrived on the scene and jumped into the skiff with Boker. Five of the men from the overturned craft were washed toward the shore by the breaking waves; Longstreet and Boker grabbed the other two. But before reaching the shore, one of the five men in the surf succumbed to the power of the sea and sank beneath the waves. Harry Anderson swam to his rescue, hauling him ashore and allowing the keeper to work on his resuscitation. After an hour of Life-Saving Service–mandated artificial resuscitation, the man responded and was revived.

Two

BAYHEAD TO
FORKED RIVER

The surfmen and keepers of the U.S. Life-Saving Service lived in castles that reflected their chivalrous actions as "storm warriors" and "heroes of the surf"—or so it sometimes seemed. Actually, the architectural styles of the country's lifesaving stations stood out simply as examples of their era in history. There was more to be said, though, of the four Deal-type stations built at Deal, Bayhead (shown here), Atlantic City, and Brenton Point (Rhode Island) between 1882 and 1885. Lifesaving stations came in two standard forms: either remote and far away from the general populace, or smack in the heart of a busy harbor. The Life-Saving Service and other branches of the federal government made a conscious effort to add to the aesthetic beauty of important communities by designing buildings that would either fit in with or enhance the structures around them. This station at Bay Head (the Life-Saving Service used "Bayhead" in its records), at the head of Barnegat Bay, epitomized the height of Life-Saving Service architecture.

Although its tower and other features had been removed by the 1920s, the Bayhead Station still functioned as a viable Coast Guard center of operations during Prohibition. Without the tower, though, it had lost its Victorian luster. A previous structure on this site held the name Point Pleasant Life-Saving Station, but the name was changed to the more recognizable one in 1883.

The later, freestanding Coast Guard watchtowers were as utilitarian in design as the old attached cupolas of the Deal-type stations were ornamental. Watchtowers like the one above at Bayhead served the country in several ways, from presiding over shipping to spying for rumrunners to watching for U-boats in World War II. The Bayhead Station, though, was last used for active service in 1937, before the coming of the war.

The crew at Bayhead Station appears in this revealing photograph. Two important features are shown here. The first is that many crews had dogs as mascots, although black Labrador retrievers usually outnumbered all other breeds. The second, seen behind the dog, is the Manby mortar, one of the earliest line-throwing guns for use with the breeches buoy rescue system used in the United States.

Two and a half miles south of Barnegat Bay, the Mantoloking Station, known until 1883 as Swan Point Life-Saving Station, was a Jersey-pattern structure. Like Bayhead Station, Mantoloking did not finish out the 1930s on the active roster. Better communications technology and higher-quality motorized lifeboats cut down the need for so many buildings. The station closed in 1938, but was not transferred to the General Services Administration until 1953.

These images, found in the Osborn collection, feature the Mantoloking crew hard at work on a breeches buoy in 1913. Above, the crew is ready to hoist a "victim" into the breeches buoy, a pair of canvas breeches sewn around a life ring and suspended from a hawser on a traveling block, or pulley. In the distance, a wreck pole mocks a ship's mast. In times of emergency, a crew ashore would fire a projectile carrying a thin rope, or line, out to a stranded or foundering ship. The endangered sailors would haul on the line to drag a medium-weight line out to the ship; then they would drag out a heavier line, the hawser. The lines carried a block, a tally board giving instructions on what to do with the lines and block, and the breeches buoy in tow. The medium-weight line, called the whip, tied to one side of the traveling block supporting the breeches buoy, ran through a pulley affixed to the mast and another anchored ashore, and then passed back to the other side of the traveling block, completing a loop that created a setup similar to a continuous clothesline. Handling the line on shore, the lifesaving crew could send the breeches buoy out to the ship and bring it back again.

The breeches buoy system was less complicated than it sounds. Every surfman had an assigned task based on his ranking in the station's hierarchy, from one to seven. Although practiced twice a week at more than 250 stations around the country, the system was used rarely—approximately 25 times a year nationwide. But until the Life-Saving Service's Board of Life-Saving Appliances and, later, the Coast Guard, could develop a better system for delivering a lifeline to a shipwreck, the breeches buoy remained the last hope of sailors trapped on ships within the breaker line. Improved technology did not arrive until the development of the helicopter in the 1930s and 1940s. Yet instances still occur today that call for the use of the breeches buoy. In the 1970s, the Coast Guard rescued a man trapped on one of the supports of the Golden Gate Bridge in San Francisco, a place where a helicopter could not go, by use of a shoulder-fired line-throwing gun and breeches buoy. Six members of the Mantoloking crew—Keeper Britton C. Miller and surfmen William H. Brower, Louis Truex, Abram J. Jones, Charles W. Flemming, and Demerest T. Herbert—earned Gold Life-Saving Medals for a heroic breeches buoy rescue performed at the wreck of the *George Taulane* on February 3, 1880.

At least once a week, in all types of weather, the men of the Life-Saving Service dragged their lifeboats out to the water's edge and took to the sea. Although some stations had horses to help pull the boats and their undercarriages to the surf, many did not. When the call "wreck ashore" rang out and the boat room doors flew open, bystanders could see the surfmen, with ropes around their chests, pulling the boats to the rescue. After doing such incredible labor across wet sands and past obstacles of all kinds, including tree branches and telephone and telegraph wires downed by the winds, the lifesavers had to board their boats and row to wrecks, sometimes remaining seaborne for hours in frigid temperatures. The Life-Saving Service first experimented with motorized lifeboats in 1899 on the Great Lakes, but these boats did not come into widespread use until about a decade later. Even so, crews kept up their rowing skills through the Great Depression. A lifeboat would be of little use in chasing rumrunners, but, like the breeches buoy, the crews never knew when it would come in handy.

Once in the water, the lifesavers took up their positions, with one man to an oar and the keeper standing at the stern with the sweep, or steering oar. On top of practicing standard craft-handling techniques, the crews purposely turned their boats over in the water and attempted to right them again. The drill was designed in preparation for the most dreaded of possibilities: an overturning during a rescue. Sadly, through the years, dozens of lifesavers lost their lives as a result of a capsizing. The lifesavers could practice in still waters all they wanted, but that could never replicate the conditions of a roiling sea and the confusion of a scattered crew groping for an overturned lifeboat. In a tragic moment on Cape Cod on March 17, 1902, all but one member of a seven-man rescue crew drowned while making a routine rescue.

Oftentimes, returning to shore from a drill or a wreck could be just as harrowing as launching into the surf. Several coastguardsmen died unexpectedly on return voyages, even during what were usually routine events. The crew at Bayhead, though, had little to fear this calm day on the water. Judging by the number of people in the boat, it is clear that this was no ordinary drill.

Offering boat rides to the public, family, or friends was perhaps the best public relations tactic the surfmen and keepers of the U.S. Life-Saving Service could have ever launched. A mother and several youngsters hop out of the surf boat on this warm summer's day.

To complete the experience, some youngsters even joined in by pulling the boats ashore with their local heroes. If these youngsters timed it correctly, the next time they returned they might have even gotten a chance to be "saved" as mock victims in the breeches buoy.

Two and a half miles south of the Mantoloking Station stood the Chadwick Life-Saving Station, another relic of the late 18th century still in service to the United States Coast Guard. In this image, it still shows the characteristic watchtower typical of 1882-type stations. This building had been expanded over the years to include the side boat room and porch. William Chadwick, a Gold Life-Saving Medal recipient, served as keeper of the stations on this site from 1868 to 1887. The building was abandoned in 1939.

On the porch of the Chadwick Station are, from left to right, the following: (first row) John Souter, unidentified, and Clem Lewis; (second row) two unidentified men, Willie Lewis, and J. Quidley.

The Jersey-type Toms River Station, located on Barnegat Barrier Island across from the mouth of the river, replaced an earlier structure. This one was completed about the time of the incorporation of Sea Side Park, as it was then called. The building served boaters in the area as a lifesaving station and a Coast Guard station for more than six decades before closing in 1964. After extensive renovations were made, the borough of Seaside Park moved its offices into the building, which still stands today. In homage to the site's past, the storage facility behind the building today holds lifeguard equipment.

The Island Beach Station shows proof of the changes in technology that brought permanent disruption to Coast Guard life. The active shoreside stations, once known for their "sandpounders," surfmen who walked the beaches every night vigilantly searching for signs of shipwrecks, began to spread farther and farther apart as radio towers and motor lifeboats arrived on scene. Although still ever-watchful for potential danger along the shore, the coastguardsmen of the 1930s had the added asset of ship-to-shore radio to alert them in times of emergency.

Nearly five and a half miles south of the Island Beach Station, the Cedar Creek Station, an original Red House type, served well into the Coast Guard years before its discontinuation as an active site in 1939. According to Ralph Shanks in *The United States Life-Saving Service: Heroes, Rescues and Architecture of the Early Coast Guard*, author Pearl Buck, who wrote *The Good Earth*, used the building as a summer home.

Built with the same Red House–type design as the Cedar Creek Station, the Forked River Station, like many early lifesaving stations along the New Jersey coast, sat on land for which no conveyance was originally made. In many instances, deed holders had moved on and left the land behind and out of their memories. This station saw its last action in 1948.

Three
BARNEGAT TO
SOUTH BRIGANTINE

The men serving with the United States Coast Guard shoreside stations in the 1930s faced challenges different than those of their predecessors in the Life-Saving Service. While some things remained the same—the constant close contact between crew mates (whether they liked each other or not), the long, drawn-out periods of relative inactivity between rescue attempts, and even the repetitive patrols along the beaches—other aspects of life at the small boat stations had forever changed. For instance, in 1872, no surfman in New Jersey had to worry about his boat exploding, simply because it had no engine attached to it. The same could not be said for the Coast Guard crew at the Barnegat Station five decades later, as evidenced by this image in the collection of Captain Osborn.

Like many other New Jersey lifesaving stations—in fact, 40 of the 41—the original Barnegat Station sat on land that had not been conveyed to the federal government. As the northernmost of the seven stations on Long Beach Island, Barnegat guarded the southern side of the approach to Barnegat Bay. The land was finally transferred in 1911, after the station had been there, in one form or another, for more than half a century.

The men at the Barnegat Station had the added vigilance of the keepers of Barnegat Lighthouse. Barnegat Light, at 161 feet tall, still stands today as one of New Jersey's most recognizable landmarks, in its own state park at the northernmost tip of Long Beach Island. The outbuildings were washed away in a storm in 1933.

The crew at Loveladies Island worked on the only land never conveyed to the federal government; the Coast Guard obtained rights for all of the other 40 stations. This 1871 Red House–type station still stands in its original location today, one of three such stations on Long Beach Island.

According to New Jersey historian and maritime author Margaret Thomas Buchholz, the community of Harvey Cedars owes its interesting name to a corruption of the name "Harvest Quarters" and not to anyone named Harvey. The first station in town was a Red House type; the Coast Guard moved to a new site in town to build a Duluth-type station in 1901. Both the Red House–type and Duluth-type buildings remain today.

Another Jersey-pattern station stood at Ship Bottom, the working home of seven Gold Life-Saving Medal recipients—Keeper Isaac W. Truex and surfmen J. Horace Cranmer, James H. Cranmer, Walter Pharo, Barton P. Pharo, A. B. Salmons, and C. V. Conklin. They were rewarded for their efforts in rescuing the crew of the barkentine *Abiel Abbot* in January 1903.

Three men—Keeper George Mathis and surfmen W. E. Pharo and M. D. Kelly—from the Long Beach Station to the south (in what is now known as Beach Haven Terrace) also earned Gold Life-Saving Medals for the *Abiel Abbot* rescue. De-commissioned in 1945, the station remains standing today.

The Bonds Life-Saving Station was moved from its original site in 1899, long before this photograph was taken. This structure, a Bibb No. 2–type station built from 1887 to 1888, survived that move away from encroaching seas, as well as a second move in the 1920s. The original site is now underwater.

The sandy patch on which the Bonds Life-Saving Station stood, easily accessible by meandering pathways, shows the remoteness of life on certain parts of Long Beach Island in the 1920s and 1930s. If the crew got along at Bonds Station, life was good. If they could not stand each other, it would be a long winter.

The isolation of life at the Little Egg Station did not reflect the community's industrious past. Shipbuilders, lumber traders, salt works owners, and even a famous duck-decoy carver all operated out of Tuckerton, which at one time was America's third port of entry. The heavy vessel traffic justified the placement of a station here in 1855, with new buildings constructed in 1872 and 1899.

The final Little Egg Life-Saving Station, still operational during the early Coast Guard years, was a Jersey-pattern structure. It remained on active service through World War II and beyond. In 1964, it was turned over to the General Services Administration for transferral either within or without the federal government. The station no longer stands.

Sometimes the lifesavers at particular stations formed their own communities out of need. They were located away from the center of town in order to best accomplish their mission; if they wanted to have their families with them, they had to provide living quarters for them. For most of the Life-Saving Service era, the surfmen worked for 10 months of the year, excluding June and July, as the winter storms were their deadliest foes. Therefore, a family could not necessarily expect to spend the summer at the Jersey Shore when a father or brother took a job with the service. In time, though, the service became a year-round job, especially as pleasure-boating increased in harbors and bays along the coast. The crew at the Quonochontaug-type Little Beach Station had ready-made housing on hand, the basis of a solid Coast Guard community.

These images of the Little Egg Station after an October 1927 nor'easter show the consequences of building so near the ocean. Especially during the pulling-boat days of the early shore-based rescue services (including volunteer organizations), stations constructed as close to the water's edge as possible were a necessity, as seconds and minutes lost while trying to get equipment to a wreck meant the difference between lives lost or saved. Later, when faster and more reliable boats became more readily available and widespread, only the boathouses needed to be in harm's way, and the station's berthing and communications areas could be pulled back to higher or regularly drier ground. This storm was so powerful that it knocked over the Little Egg Harbor Lighthouse. The entire island upon which it sat, Tucker's Island, the area's first summer resort, has since been washed away.

These scenes of destruction from the 1927 storm were just the prelude to a 1932 storm that sent breaking waves bashing against the doors and walls of the Little Egg Station. Eventually, due to the danger, the coastguardsmen had to flee their station for safer ground elsewhere.

Both the 1927 and the 1932 storms did their fair share of damage to the local surroundings, as evidenced by the discombobulation seen here at the Little Egg Harbor docks after the former tempest. Water rushed down the streets from the beach side, while occupants of houses on the bay side fled to higher ground in the face of water coming from the other direction.

If they were not there before the surfmen arrived, well-trodden paths through the scrub growth near the stations along the New Jersey shore were soon developed by the lifesavers on their nightly patrols. Even into the Depression era, and for different purposes during World War II, a man on foot with a lantern and a flare was still an effective tool in the quest to save lives at sea. This well-kept path leads to the door of the Little Beach Station.

Dressing up for a photograph was not every coastguardsman's idea of a good time. Some lighthouse keepers on remote stations hated the idea of inspections, but not because of the way they kept their lights. They enjoyed their isolation and the freedom of life on "island time," and they disliked the formality of district inspectors. Much the same could be said for some of the front-line men of the surf stations of the Coast Guard. We can only surmise through facial expressions what the crew at Little Beach thought of Captain Osborn's arrival.

South of Little Beach Station and north of South Brigantine Station sat Brigantine Station. This Jersey-pattern station had been moved from a previous location, like many others, due to a storm in 1888. Unlike other New Jersey stations, however, Brigantine did not have a Red House station built between its early 1849 station and its 1898–1899 Jersey-pattern structure.

When times were slow, routine maintenance became the word of the day. Drills could only take so much time each morning or afternoon, so keepers had to find something to occupy the hands and minds of the crews. Painting the watchtower, which was more than 60 feet tall, was quite a task at the Brigantine Station.

Developers and city planners had already laid the groundwork for the expected growth of the area around the station at South Brigantine. Located one and a quarter miles north of Absecon Lighthouse in Atlantic City, it guarded the northern side of the entry to Absecon Inlet. This 1882-type structure, built in 1883, has not survived.

Lifesaving crews located at the ends of peninsulas or otherwise isolated from other stations walked their patrols just like any other crew. But instead of meeting another surfman from an adjacent station and exchanging "checks"—small identifying brass tags—they used key posts and patrolmen's clocks to mark their time, proving to their keepers that they had walked the entire beat out and back. The men at South Brigantine would have used just such a system.

Four

ATLANTIC CITY
TO TOWNSEND INLET

In 2004, Atlantic City celebrated its sesquicentennial, 150 years of cityhood, but its earliest European-descended settlers had arrived on Absecon Island well before the city's establishment. Jeremiah Leeds built the first permanent dwelling on the island in 1785. In Massachusetts, a group of philanthropic-minded individuals met that same year to discuss the formation of an organization predicated on the search for new technology and methodologies regarding the resuscitation of the apparently drowned. This group, the Humane Society of the Commonwealth of Massachusetts, later entered the world of organized shore-based lifesaving of mariners in distress, becoming a template for other regional systems and, eventually, a federal lifesaving system. As early as 1855, that national organization, the predecessor of the United States Life-Saving Service, built a station in Atlantic City. Seen here is a classic example of an 1872 Red House–type lifesaving station still standing in Atlantic City in 1930, a relic of the bygone days of pulling boats and sailing ships, yet still in service during the war on demon rum.

The crew at Atlantic City chased rumrunners in its 36-foot-long Type H motor lifeboat. The Type H boats, which replaced the Type E class, displayed distinctive engine compartments at their center, or amidship. Although sturdy and seaworthy, 36-footers struggled to keep up with the rumrunners' high-speed boats. If coastguardsmen captured a rummy "go-fast," as it would be termed today, they repainted it and pressed it into service chasing its former owners.

In a more formal scene, the crew of the Atlantic City Coast Guard Station poses outside the boat room doors. Lifesaving station crews traditionally consisted of seven or eight men: six or seven surfmen and a keeper. By the 1930s, crews had grown, but not to the point where manpower alone would win the war on rum.

Built in 1856, Absecon Lighthouse still stands today at the corner of Pacific and Rhode Island Avenues on the great Monopoly board that is Atlantic City. De-commissioned in 1932, it is now a museum. At 171 feet tall, the lighthouse provides quite a hike from floor to lantern room. Working alongside the Coast Guard stations, the lighthouse shared in lifesaving for many years. The Atlantic City Coast Guard Station, located on Vermont Avenue, can be seen to the right of the lighthouse in this aerial photograph.

Although it no longer exists today, the station is still interpreted by signs at the Absecon Lighthouse site. Originally on the shore, the lighthouse and the lifesaving station unwittingly moved farther inland as sand was deposited on the island. Today the lighthouse is a half mile from the shore.

47

Farther down Absecon Island, two and three-quarter miles south of Absecon Lighthouse, the Absecon Life-Saving Station remained in service during Prohibition. Built in the sturdy Duluth type, a class named for the first structure of its type built in Duluth, Minnesota, in 1894, the Absecon Station replaced an earlier 1871 Red House–type structure. Built in 1896, the Absecon Station stood at a crossroads of Coast Guard architecture. Not quite old enough to be torn down by the 1930s, the station stood by as the Coast Guard entered a new era of construction during the Depression. Several Duluth-type stations, including this one, remain today.

Six and three-quarter miles south of Absecon Lighthouse, the Great Egg Life-Saving Station guarded the northern approach to Great Egg Harbor Inlet. Known as a Bibb No. 2–type station after its designer, Albert B. Bibb, the 1888 Great Egg Station no longer stands, though similar structures elsewhere in New Jersey, Rhode Island, and along the south shore of Massachusetts stand in excellent condition.

A crew poses outside of its station. Captain Osborn did his best to record the names of the crew members, but for this image he could only identify three men: C. Turner (the first man on the left in the first row), ? Henderson (third from the left in the first row), and Foster Waddell (second from the right in the second row). Until the use of the civil service examination system began in the later years of the Life-Saving Service, crews were drawn from local populations, and men served for several years at the same station. After 1896, they moved within the district.

The lifesaving station at Ocean City, New Jersey (not to be confused with the station at Ocean City, Maryland), once stood guard on the shore. It was identified by its large flagpole, its wide roof with cupola, and its station number, 126. (Numbers were assigned beginning in Maine and proceeding down the coast.) But, like its counterpart in Atlantic City, the station has retreated from the shoreline as sand has accumulated along the coast. Today the station is listed by the U.S. Life-Saving Service Heritage Association as one of the most endangered buildings of its type in the nation, as a developer plans to tear it down. A collaborative effort is underway by several local preservation and historical groups to save the structure under the name of the Save Our Station Coalition.

A small Ocean City crew turned out for this photograph. They are, from left to right, the following: (first row) J. Emory, F. Parker, and unidentified; (second row) R. F. Peterson, Roy Merrill, and unidentified. The traditional crew of a surf station consisted of a keeper and seven surfmen, ranked one through seven, usually by seniority. Some stations around the country added an extra seasonal surfman in the coldest months, someone to share the load of patrols and drills when the weather was at its worst. Duties included, first and foremost, patrolling the beaches for shipwrecks and sitting in the watchtower, with each task performed in four-hour watches. Surfmen also took turns cooking for the entire crew, drilled five days a week, kept the station clean, and even responded to non-shipwreck emergencies in the communities in which they worked, including fires. Not much had changed in the daily life of the surfman by the 1930s.

Shown here from the air, Peck's Beach Station, number 127, was south of Ocean City and slightly more than eight miles north of Corson Inlet. The Life-Saving Service had come a long way architecturally from its earliest days by 1899, when this station was built.

Photographs in the National Archives and the United States Coast Guard Historian's office mirror this view into the past. The revered old station keeper, surrounded by his younger, stronger crew, was motif number one during the Life-Saving Service years. That tradition had not died by the 1930s.

The Jersey-pattern stations, designed by architect Victor Mendelheff and built between 1898 and 1900, did not only appear in New Jersey. One Jersey-pattern stood watch over the coastline at Hampton Beach, New Hampshire, while a modified design appeared in Cleveland, Ohio. The station type featured a tall, octagonal watchtower, ample boat-room storage and wide access points, and spacious crew accommodations. During the early years of the Life-Saving Service, stations barely had room for their equipment. In time, during the Coast Guard construction wave of the 1930s, stations were separated from boathouses and other utility buildings, and watchtowers eventually became architectural details of the past. The tall, reinforced flagpole stands at the right as the crew gathers around the doorway at Peck's Beach.

Seen from the air and shown from the back, the Corson Inlet Station, designated number 128, looks like just another house along the Jersey shoreline, yet inside lived and worked the men of the Coast Guard. Originally on 58th Street Beach in Ocean City, the station was moved in 1924 to Strathmere Bay. The relocation allowed for the construction of a boathouse and launchway appropriate for motorized craft.

An 1899 Jersey-pattern structure, the Corson Inlet Station featured the imposing watchtower of the other similarly styled stations along the coast, but after its move, the boat room was no longer housed within it. This building still stands today as a private home. Across the street, the attendant boathouse remains as well, though in rather rough condition.

The Coast Guard station at Sea Isle City, number 129, sat three and one-half miles north of Townsend Inlet, between a boardwalk and a billboard. This station was originally designated Ludlam's Beach Life-Saving Station.

Another standard, trustworthy Bibb No. 2–type station, the Sea Isle City Station, built in 1888, still stands today.

As the new Life-Saving Service expanded in 1878, freshly broken away from the Revenue Marine (with which it would later reunite to form the Coast Guard), new stations were built along the coast. Land for a station at Townsend Inlet was purchased in 1878, and a new site was purchased in 1885. This Bibb No. 2–type station was built between 1886 and 1887.

Later, in 1906, the Life-Saving Service and the borough of Townsend Inlet faced a roadblock. The station did not sit squarely on the purchased lot as intended; instead, it blocked the construction of two proposed roadways. After some creative political problem-solving, the block was redefined and the station and the thoroughfares lived in harmony.

Five

AVALON TO CAPE MAY

When the United States Life-Saving Service realized that the station built at Avalon on Seven Mile Beach was not on high enough ground, the group abandoned the original building and built this Duluth-type structure on new land in 1894. Abandoned in 1948, the building is now a private home. Deep within its walls, though, live the memories of four brave lifesavers who earned gold medals for the rescue of the crew of the seagoing tug *Margaret* in December 1912.

Another Duluth-type station stood midway between Avalon and the Hereford Inlet Lighthouse at Stone Harbo (previously known as Tatham's Life-Saving Station). Eight men from the Stone Harbor Station also earned Gold Life-Saving Medals for their actions during the rescue of the tug *Margaret*. Under a howling wind, the combined crews rescued 10 men from the crippled craft.

By 1930, only the locals would have remembered the heroism of the Avalon and Stone Harbor crews, but the story would no doubt have been passed down to the young men occupying the Stone Harbor Station in years to come. Although the men came from scattered points around the United States, unit pride, like that seen today, existed in the 1930s Coast Guard.

The Bibb No. 2–type Hereford Inlet Station has come and gone. Even before it was built in 1888, the Life-Saving Service had moved its predecessor, built in 1849, away from the encroaching sea. This structure, one of 22 of its type built from New Jersey to New Hampshire (and one of nine in New Jersey), was constructed on land adjoining the Hereford Inlet Lighthouse. The photographer did a good job of almost completely blocking the lighthouse out of the shot, but some details are visible.

The 1930 crew of the Hereford Inlet Station was comprised of the following men, seen here from left to right: (first row) C. Wright, J. Freeman, H. Chadwick, and J. Mathis; (second row) G. Burrus, R. Pool, unidentified, ? Palmer, and A. Willis. In a few years, they would move into a new Roosevelt-type building. Today, that building is used by the New Jersey Marine State Police. The lighthouse remains as well, open to the public as a museum in North Wildwood.

The Holly Beach Station, known after 1899 as Wildwood Life-Saving Station, was abandoned just after the end of World War II, in 1946. Yet another Jersey-pattern structure, it has not survived into the modern day.

Although some Red House–type stations were still in use in the 1930s, the station at Two Mile Beach, four miles northeast of Cape May City, had seen its best days pass by.

Not that long ago, a Coast Guard crew—and its faithful mutt—occupied the Cold Spring Beach Station. Visitors to the site today would not believe their eyes. Today, the Cold Spring Beach structure, a Bibb No. 2 type, sits amongst the hotels, motels, and amusements of Cape May, dwarfed by buildings on both sides. The building is still just a few feet away from the ocean across Beach Street, but its current residents are not as keen on watching the waves as their predecessors. The station is now home to the Cape May Kiwanis Club.

These men appear outside the 1930s Cold Spring Beach Station. Pictured, from left to right, are the following: (first row) two unidentified men, K. Redgraves, and R. O'Neil; (second row) C. L. Lewis, two unidentified men, and William Burton.

By the 1930s, the Coast Guard's architectural plans for lifeboat stations had taken a turn onto a very straight and narrow road. Although Roosevelt-type stations, with their Colonial Revival style, would stand out in the 1930s (many are still in use around the United States today), structures like this one at Cold Spring would define the Coast Guard's future.

Whether the men (and, later, women) of the Coast Guard operated out of flashy buildings of Victorian or Gothic styles or out of utilitarian structures, they still performed the same duties they always did, "saving lives and property."

Cape May Point saw the construction of its first lifesaving station in 1849. That station, due to the advancing seas, moved several times. A second station, built in 1876 for the Philadelphia Centennial Exhibition, was moved to Cape May after the celebration. Finally, in 1896, a Duluth-type station was built at the point. The Cape May Lighthouse is just out of view to the right.

In 1924, the lifeboat crew at Cape May Point witnessed the birth of one of the Coast Guard's earliest air facilities, as land taken over from the navy that year became a Coast Guard air base. By 1948, the Coast Guard had made Cape May the home of its east coast recruit training, and in 1982, the service consolidated all of its recruit training there, the southernmost point in New Jersey.

The Coast Guard still knew, though, that even with the arrival of manned flight technology in 1903, its main mission would always be to serve mariners in distress on the sea, and the best way to fulfill that mission would be from a seagoing platform.

The crew at Cape May Point practices the skill that made the Life-Saving Service famous: launching a surf boat into the sea. After wheeling it to the water's edge, the coastguardsmen will break away the carriage underneath and set the boat afloat.

With each man in his assigned position, the boat will head seaward for a day's drill. Competent oarsmen like those of the Life-Saving Service and Coast Guard learned to time the breaking waves, waiting for a natural lull before making their charge. With a good, sturdy man at the sweep, or steering oar, the crew could rest assured in the knowledge that, even while facing the stern in order to pull the boat in the right direction, they would be safe.

Until the invention of motorized lifeboats, heading up and over the crashing surf was the most direct path to a shipwreck for the men of the U.S. Life-Saving Service. Although today's Coast Guard lifeboats do not launch directly into heavy seas like the pulling surf boats of yore, the service still trains its coxswains to face such conditions in storms and surges. The instructors at the National Motor Lifeboat School in Ilwaco, Washington, teach their students—many of whom are training to be surfman-qualified, a designation revived in honor of the old lifesavers—how to handle heavy seas on the Columbia River Bar, known as the most dangerous stretch of water in the world. For the men of the Life-Saving Service and early Coast Guard in New Jersey, it was all in a day's work.

Six
RUMRUNNING TALES

The cry for the national prohibition of alcohol had been gaining volume for more than a century before the adoption of the 18th Amendment by Congress and its eventual ratification by the 36th and deciding state, Nebraska, on January 14, 1919. The passage of the Volstead Act in October 1919, over the veto of Pres. Woodrow Wilson, charted the course for the Coast Guard's short-term future. The administration of the law fell to the Bureau of Internal Revenue, a sibling agency of the Coast Guard under the umbrella of the Department of the Treasury. America officially went "dry" for the first time on January 17, 1920. January 17 was no Fourth of July, but on that historic day, the fireworks began.

As stated by Malcolm F. Willoughby in *Rum War at Sea*, "Liquor came from three principal sources. There was that manufactured in many thousands of homes; that which was produced in thousands of stills, chiefly in the back country but also in cities and towns; and that which entered the country from outside its borders." The Coast Guard focused its efforts on the third source, as evidenced by this capture on Michigan's Detroit River in the summer of 1929.

New Jersey quickly became one of the most strategic points of entry for rumrunners bringing illegal liquor onto American shores, as well as one of the most important points of defense for the coastguardsmen trying to stop that flow. Captures like this one at Seabright became common up and down the barrier islands.

Because of its proximity to New York City and its underworld and to millions of potential customers, the offshore flotilla of cargo ships known as Rum Row stretched itself from the waters off Long Island down the coast of New Jersey. Rumrunners (those lucky enough to avoid capture by the Coast Guard, unlike the owners of this boat) met the ships offshore, loaded up with as much as they could, and took off for shore under the cover of darkness.

Coastguardsmen did all they could to staunch the flow of liquor to the area, but with thousands of miles of coastline to guard and a relatively thin corps of men to do the work, rumrunners found many gaps through which to pass. Also, with only a three-mile zone to cross between international waters and shore, a boat faster than a Coast Guard lifeboat, patrol boat, or picket boat could simply outrun its pursuers.

The international water zone was eventually pushed back to 12 miles from shore. When that happened, the rumrunners sought bigger, faster boats. As the Coast Guard tried to follow suit, the rumrunners always stayed one step ahead, spending their ill-gotten money at boat yards for the promise of top-of-the-line equipment.

Speed could not help the *Monolola* when it ended up deep in the sand at Jones Beach on Long Island. The Coast Guard moved in quickly to unload its quarry and document what it found for use in later legal proceedings.

Booze came ashore in various styles of packaging. Some came in barrels, some in boxes, and still more in "sacks" purportedly invented by Bill McCoy, the subject of the slang expression, "It's the real McCoy." When asked if his stuff was any good, he would respond that of course it was, it was "the real McCoy" after all. His sacks consisted of three bottles on the bottom, two stacked on top of them, and one more atop that, a system that he—and many others—considered perfect for hauling hooch. No doubt the coastguardsmen who had to off-load untold sacks from the dozens and dozens of rumrunners they stopped thanked him for his genius, as it made their jobs easier as well.

The *K-13535*, low and fast and loaded to the gunwales with alcohol, had nowhere to hide its banned cargo when it was stopped and seized by the Coast Guard on December 17, 1928, off Seabright. Towed ashore with its payload, the vessel awaited an uncertain fate. But as the speed war gained momentum, the Coast Guard learned that, as the old adage said, it should fight fire with fire.

In order to beat the rumrunners at their own game, the Coast Guard adopted the practice of converting captured rum boats, especially the faster craft, for national service. Once on the foul side of the law, they became the best weapons the law could have. The Coast Guard converted hundreds of such vessels from 1925 to 1935, replacing their names with the letters "CG" and an identifying number.

In the great cat-and-mouse game that the undeclared war became, in which rumrunners and "coasties" waved hello to each other by day and chased and shot at each other through the night, the playing field became somewhat leveled through the process of converting captured rum boats.

Late in the 19th century, the world of boat and ship names took a sad turn away from tradition. Gone were the days of *Flying Cloud*; in were the days of *Louise*. The romance of the sea had been lost forever (unless there is something we do not know about Louise), and the practice of naming boats for family members had taken over. Of course, the simple tactic of changing vessel names to avoid leaving a paper trail was as old as life itself, and it still goes on today among the pirates of the Far East and African coasts, who hijack tankers and cargo carriers and resell them under new appellations. *Louise* may once have been *Mary* or maybe even *Flying Cloud*. Some rumrunners went as far as to paint their boats one color on one side and an opposite color on the other side. When they went out fishing, lobstering, or oystering in the morning, if under suspicion, they presented a certain look. Later, when the Coast Guard watched for their return, the boat would look different.

Smuggling was once as American as George Washington's cherry tree. During the American Revolution, political leaders encouraged it; however, after the Revolution had ended, they frowned upon it, as the country needed all the revenue it could get and smuggled goods meant less tax dollars for the young republic. The modern Coast Guard traces its roots to the Revenue Cutter Service, founded specifically to collect import duties on goods brought to American shores.

Smuggling was in the blood of many American rumrunners when the country went dry in 1920, not that many generations removed from the founding fathers. Unfortunately, even after the repeal of Prohibition in December 1933, smugglers kept up their trade. They just shifted their focus from alcohol to narcotics, pushing the United States to places it had never been before.

The Coast Guard's modern war on drugs mirrors the war on rum in many ways, most notably in the high-speed pursuits and the use of weaponry by the service in stopping its elusive prey. In the days leading up to the terrorist attacks on the World Trade Center and the Pentagon on September 11, 2001, the hottest debate in Coast Guard circles centered on whether or not the service should arm the helicopters that were fighting the war on drugs. Proponents of the use of weapons pointed out that a single well-placed sniper shot could cripple an engine on a "go-fast" boat, or a burst of fire from a machine gun across the bow could cause a drug runner to think twice—a practice used successfully in the 1920s and 1930s. Opponents stated that the Coast Guard is supposed to save lives, not endanger them. After the terrorist attacks of 2001, the sight of a port security detail with bow- and stern-mounted machine guns became commonplace all around the United States, and the argument about helicopters entirely disappeared.

The notion that the Coast Guard was fighting a "war" on rum may sound like hyperbolic symbolism, but the fact was that many people died of bullet wounds and other related "warlike" injuries. By the end of 1920, one civilian and one federal agent had been killed in Prohibition-related confrontations. By April 1926, according to Malcolm Willoughby's *Rum War at Sea,* 89 civilians and 47 federal employees, including two coastguardsmen, had died. By 1930, those numbers had risen to 200 civilians and 86 agents, and none of those numbers reflected state or local officials and their run-ins. Boats were crashed, shots were fired, and lives were lost. The result of Prohibition may not have been on a grand scale, but for a country supposedly at peace, portions of the United States at times looked like a war zone.

The allure of quick money tempted coastguardsmen to accept bribes (in cash or liquid assets), protect known rumrunners, or even leave the service and join the anti-establishment side of the war. Very few cases of coastguardsmen conspiring to aid the rumrunners ever reached the country's courts, but a few men did fall prey to that particular siren's song.

Part of the problem was that the coastguardsmen who worked the harbors and bays all day long knew the locals very well, and the locals knew them just as well. High school classmates could be on either side of a chase, based on their position for or against Prohibition. Boats that were well known to all went from local mainstay to public enemy overnight on January 17, 1920.

The skipper of the *Roenomore* had more to worry about than his early days spent bent over an oar. Caught red-handed with a boatload of booze, he faced an uncertain future, his fate most likely to be decided by a judge.

If a captured vessel was not fit for service to the Coast Guard, it did not survive much longer, as the service burned and destroyed many rumrunning boats.

"G" for gin was a simple way to remember what was contained in each sack when it came time to off-load in a hurry.

In the midst of all the unpleasant happenings of the Prohibition years, the Coast Guard continued to save lives. According to Captain Osborn, "Two boys from Maine started off for the West Indies in this yawl in bad condition; got tangled up in pound fish net off Chadwick's assisted by CG and towed to Hubert Johnson boat works at Bayhead. Claimed the boat, launched it, stopped near Manasquan Inlet, robbed two cottages in Bay Head at night and started to sea with the booty. Were caught by CG at Sandy Hook."

The Coast Guard's chase after illegal liquor did not necessarily stop once the booze hit the shore. As federal agents, they watched and listened for tips about the locations of transfer sites and drop-off points as well.

Due to the sometimes poor quality of the moonshine and home-distilled gin flowing in the United States, Bermudan, Canadian, and European liquor became highly sought after. Some unscrupulous dealers sold rotgut that caused blindness in some unsuspecting victims who were just out to get their fix. Prohibition brought out the worst in some of America's citizens.

As the war continued, the cache of war prizes continued to grow. On June 4, 1930, the Coast Guard seized this overloaded boat, along with its cargo, and brought it into Atlantic City.

Captain Osborn (second from the right, in civilian clothing) must have been proud of the men of the Fourth District, as from station to station he found more and more evidence of their success in capturing breakers of the Prohibition law.

Working out of the Seabright Station, the crew of the CG 2236 took credit for the capture of the K-13535, formerly known as the Sachem, in December 1928.

The crew at Little Egg Inlet captured the Malba and brought her crew to justice.

It took 14 years, but the nation finally changed its collective mind about the prohibition of alcohol. Mired in the Depression, in the doldrums of December 1933, the United States repealed the 18th Amendment, once again allowing liquor to flow legally down the throats of American citizens. Hundreds of people had died during the life of the "Noble Experiment," some would say needlessly. The Coast Guard suffered a tremendous beating to its once-untarnished reputation, one that still has not completely healed. Americans have long memories, and those that lost loved ones to the country's second civil war may never forget.

As with normal warfare, technology adapted for specific advantages in the field forever changed life after the war on rum ended. Small boats had become faster, perhaps prematurely, and thousands of coastguardsmen—and rumrunners—had become excellent small-boat handlers. Who knows how many ex-rumrunners ended up driving small landing craft and Higgins boats to the beaches of the South Pacific during World War II? We know that the navy called upon the men of the Coast Guard to do so throughout the conflict. The rumrunners had pulled every trick they knew, and the Coast Guard had figured out many, if not all, of them.

When the war on rum ended with no decisive winner, the United States underwent a significant change. Suspicions were dropped, guns were silenced, and the seashore grew quiet once again. According to Captain Osborn, the *Ruby* of Essex, Connecticut, was the last of the rumrunners. "One of several laid up in Morton Johnson's boat yard at Bayhead. Finally bought and altered as a yacht by some New Yorkers. Sailed with a new French name and the last I heard of her she was taken in tow by the Shark River CG, having broken down with motor trouble." Like the *Ruby*, the country's attempt at total abstinence had finally sputtered and died.

Seven
NOT NECESSARILY
NEW JERSEY

Captain Osborn's responsibilities took him away from the New Jersey shore from time to time, sometimes back to his native Long Island and sometimes to other exotic locations. Everywhere he went, though, either he or an aide snapped photographs of Coast Guard facilities, crews, and equipment, the result being an album full of varied imagery wrapped around a central Coast Guard theme. The crew at the Hog Island Station on the eastern shore of Virginia in the 1930s already knew what you, the reader, are about to find out in the upcoming few pages.

The first Hog Island Station (an 1876 type that, oddly, was built in 1875) had been washed away by beach migration by the late 1890s and was replaced with this Duluth-type station between 1897 and 1898. Sadly, this station met a similar fate.

Like many other lifesaving stations and lighthouses around the United States, the Hog Island Station sat perilously close to the water's edge. As geological changes occurred over time, with the shifting, retreating, and advancing sands reshaping beaches along the coast, some buildings succumbed to Mother Nature's will.

The Hog Island Station survived this encroaching tide mostly intact, but its best days were gone. The Coast Guard replaced it with a Chatham-type structure, a classification named for the primary building of its type, which was constructed in Chatham on Cape Cod, Massachusetts, before 1933. Ironically, the other Hog Island Station, on Long Island, was destroyed in an 1892 storm while being moved.

In the coming years, when motorized boats finally triumphed over pulling boats and launches could be made from protected waters that connected to the open sea by way of navigable inlets, station sites migrated to locations with less potential danger.

The move to less dangerous locations took place too late for the buildings at Hog Island, although a second station, Little Machipongo, opened on the north side of the island in a safer area in the late 1930s. That one had no trouble with advancing tides. Instead, it burned down.

Destroyed buildings along the waterfront were not new news for the people of New Jersey. This house fell in a 1927 storm, presumably the same one that toppled the Little Egg Harbor Lighthouse.

The owner of this house at Point Pleasant Beach at Bayhead saved it by building it on piles, but since his land had all washed away, the dwelling lost most of its value. According to Captain Osborn, "The cost to lower it was too expensive. I think he later gave it away."

The same storm that left the bungalow owner high and dry significantly damaged Point Pleasant's largest hotel, the Leighton, in September 1928. Captain Osborn stated, "The part fronting the beach was washed out and blown away, and the building split cleanly down the whole five stories. The part left standing is still in use."

Whereas a stranded sailor on a barrier island in New Jersey in the late 1800s might perish of hypothermia and exposure to the cold, a victim of a Florida shipwreck might die from dehydration and other heat-related maladies. The Life-Saving Service, understanding this situation, built several minimally manned houses of refuge along the Florida coast, including this inviting structure with the uninviting name of Mosquito Lagoon House of Refuge.

This expanded Chatham-type station stood at Kill Devils Hill on the Outer Banks of North Carolina. Just three decades earlier, two members of the Kill Devils Hill Life-Saving Station crew had participated in a significant event in world history. They had aided in the Wright Brothers' historic 1903 flight at Kitty Hawk, just to the north.

92

Far down the boardwalk at Ocean City, Maryland, overlooking the rushing waters of Assateague Inlet, the Ocean City Life-Saving Station stands today as a museum, a monument to life along the Maryland shore through time. Apart from artifacts connected to the Life-Saving Service, the museum also holds collections of salvaged artifacts from shipwrecks, a saltwater aquarium, a collection of historic bathing costumes, and more.

Farther south, the Pope's Island Life-Saving Station stood watch over the waters off Assateague Island along with three other structures. Vandals eventually got to this building after its abandonment by the Coast Guard, burning it down in 1970.

Ironically, the federal government, the body that once designed, built, staffed, and operated the station at Wallops Island, Virginia, is the same body that now endangers its existence. An 1882-type station at Wallops Island was replaced by this Depression-era lifeboat station, which remained active through the end of World War II. Although the building is in relatively good condition and has been open to the public through its current owner, the National Aeronautical and Space Administration, NASA announced in 2003 plans to destroy the building. This photograph, taken in August 1937, shows the station as new and active.

Without any identifying information or noticeable structures around it, this building is impossible to locate. During the mid-1930s, the Coast Guard began a wave of station-building that ringed the country, from New England to the Pacific Northwest and all around the Great Lakes. The design of choice, in classy Colonial Revival style, earned the name Roosevelt type for the country's four-term president, who was in office when the construction period began. The main station buildings were supported by various outbuildings, including boathouses and other utility structures. The two-and-a-half-story buildings, with cupolas that became less functional over time, represented the change from lifesaving stations to lifeboat stations in Coast Guard lingo. Several New Jersey stations gave way to Roosevelt-types in the 1930s. An example still in use today at Hereford Inlet is the New Jersey State Marine Police Station. Another well-kept example stands at Lewes, Delaware, just across Delaware Bay from Cape May.

The sea can surprise shore dwellers from time to time, and not just with its occasional surges and voyages down city streets. Sometimes it tosses an item of interest onto dry land, to the delight of beachcombers (informal, recreational finders of beach memorabilia), wreckers (people paid to help salvage a stranded ship), and mooncussers (shore-based pirates who drew unwitting ships' crews to their untimely deaths to get at their cargo) alike. Although the ship's figurehead standing on the porch behind Capt. John Lott Dorset and his little friend did not necessarily start out in New Jersey, it ended up there, for a while anyway. In Captain Osborn's words, written on the back of the original photograph, it was a "[f]igure head of wrecked ship stranded near Mantoloking. This figurehead washed over into Barnegat Bay and into Beaverdam Creek where it was taken by Captain John Lott Dorset and preserved on the porch of his house until his death. It was purchased and removed to Barnegat City and later washed out to sea when last owner's house and collection of sea relics also went."

Captain Osborn's collection did not end with the surf stations and crews of the Coast Guard on the New Jersey coast in the 1930s, but it did not go much farther than that, either. Occasionally, a photograph pops up that does not necessarily fit any category defined by the rest of the imagery, like this drill team, possibly at Midway, New Jersey, looking fine in spats and brass-buttoned shirts. It was almost as if Captain Osborn had just a few shots to spare and ran out his film on subjects he felt needed to be captured for all time as part of his personal collection.

Sometimes, the bones of the past could resurface when least expected, as did the remains of the *Civitas Correra*, which was wrecked off Squan Beach on June 28, 1888. The remnants showed up again in 1937, just in time to be documented by Captain Osborn.

Other ships wrecked in time to be captured on film but too quickly for Captain Osborn to get their names. This unidentified three-masted vessel went down somewhere off New Jersey sometime during the period of Captain Osborn's life in which he knew how to operate a camera.

Since attaching the first motor to a boat in 1899, the Coast Guard has expanded its fleet tremendously, operating everything from 21-foot-long rigid hull inflatable boats to 460-foot-long icebreakers. Anything under 65 feet is classified as a boat, while anything 65 feet and longer is considered a cutter, the traditional classification given to ships of the Revenue Cutter Service. Although 47-foot-long motor lifeboats and 41-foot-long utility boats have been standard throughout the country, smaller boats have never been standardized, especially in recent years. With today's quick rotation period for coxswains—who move in and out of stations, on average, every three years—a lot of retraining has to take place for familiarization with not only the local areas of responsibility, but with new boats as well. Here, in the 1930s, two crews of the Fourth Coast Guard District, the state of New Jersey, blast along in their search-and-rescue small craft.

What could be said of the men of the Coast Guard in the 1930s? Many of them were foreign-born, for starters, and many of them also could be considered to be some of the toughest men around. Already possessed of a willingness to risk their own lives to save others, they had also signed on for the task of chasing down and apprehending some of America's most notorious criminals in the rumrunning of the day. Captain Osborn, standing at left, knew a good crew when he saw one.

What did it take to get a young man to join the Coast Guard in the 1920s or 30s? Were the tales of the heroes of the Life-Saving Service enough to whet an appetite for adventure, or did it take more than that? Would a chance to ride in the breeches buoy and actually see lifesavers practicing their skills push the right buttons? Or was it simply the idea of job security during the Great Depression that drove a young man to sign up? We would have to ask today's young coasties what it was that pushed them to serve their country, then translate their thoughts back to a different time and place.

One thing is for sure, though: America's lifesavers just keep on coming, and heroes are born with every generation. Levin J. Bunting Jr. earned a Gold Life-Saving Medal from the Coast Guard for his actions on August 5, 1924. A 19-year-old girl was bathing offshore from the Coast Guard station at Ocean City, MD. Around 3:30 PM, Bunting, then on watch duty, heard cries for help and saw the girl struggling in the water about 75 feet from shore. She was near a jetty in a heavy surf. Bunting immediately dived into the water and succeeded in reaching the girl as she was sinking. She was brought ashore in an unconscious condition, but was soon revived. Surfman Bunting performed another gallant rescue not long after the above-mentioned case. On August 22, 1924, he saved the life of a woman bather near the Ocean City station as she was being carried out to sea by the ebbing tide. On this occasion there was a very strong outgoing current and a heavy surf. In view of this, it is considered that Bunting displayed a high degree of courage in plunging into the sea and bringing the woman ashore. Bunting received his medal on January 16, 1930.

Eight

TO SAVE LIVES
AND PROPERTY

Up until the passage of the Volstead Act, the men of the Coast Guard held a prominent spot in America's heart. As the country's storm fighters and heroes of the surf, they stood out on the front covers of national news magazines like *Harper's Weekly* and *Frank Leslie's Illustrated* in a time before rock stars and athletes wrestled the spotlight onto themselves for arguably lesser achievements in life. With Prohibition, however, the country's perception of the Coast Guard changed. Tasked with enforcing unpopular legislation, the men of the Coast Guard became vilified for simply doing their duty. Drivers of picket boats, like the 36-footer shown here in the back with a captured rumrunning craft, faced the wrath of the average American citizen for stopping the flow of liquor onto our shores. Still, with all the political tension of the Prohibition era, the men of the shoreside stations maintained a focus on their primary mission of saving lives.

S.S. MOHAWK ASHORE AT SEA BRIGHT, N.J.   COLE & C. 3885

The name *Mohawk* did not serve the Clyde Line well. On January 2, 1925, a passenger steamer named *Mohawk* caught fire off Lewes, Delaware. A second Clyde Line *Mohawk*, shown here, was stranded off Seabright, New Jersey, in the early 1930s. That same ship, launched in October 1925, later met a tragic fate. Leased by the Ward Line after the *Morro Castle* caught fire off Asbury Park, killing 124 people, the *Mohawk* left New York on January 24, 1935. Later that night, a steering malfunction forced the crew to switch to manual operation, and in the confusion, the ship made a hard turn to port, right into the path of the oncoming freighter *Talisman*. Unable to avoid the passenger ship, the *Talisman* rammed the *Mohawk*. A total of 45 of the 160 people on the steamship died in the collision, including the captain. The ship sank as the Coast Guard searched first for survivors, then for bodies. Today, the site where the *Mohawk* went down is a popular diving spot off the coast.

Ships that wreck only to sail again do not become nearly as famous as those that meet their ultimate doom on shore. This ship, unnamed in Captain Osborn's notes, ran aground north of Toms River sometime in 1910. It was surely a spectacle, as the age of sail had just about ended.

This vessel, stranded off Chadwick in 1910, is also unnamed in Captain Osborn's photograph album. It, too, was refloated and has left no significant story, at least not one that the owner of the photograph cared to pass on.

Oftentimes, once the age of sail had passed, there was nothing the Coast Guard could do to tend to a ship in need. At 2 a.m. on November 18, 1925, the 399-foot-long Clyde Line steamship *Lenape* burst into flames off the Delaware Breakwater. Built in 1913, the ship met its doom that day, burning until it was completely unsalvageable.

Once majestic and proud, the *Lenape* was reduced to a burning hulk and was finally broken up for scrap. Here, its charred remains smolder.

Boiler explosions on steamships were as old as steamships themselves. Sadly, engine-driven vessels such as coastal steamers, tugboats, and freighters introduced a new form of destruction to the ocean when they caught fire and went down. When they did, they brought their fuel with them, polluting the environment in ways not fully understood until the latter half of the 20th century.

By the 1930s, with the strength of motor lifeboats and well-trained crews to handle them, the Coast Guard had the capability to pull crews from around the country to aid faraway regions in times of natural disaster and emergency. Such practices had occurred on a small scale earlier in the century and even in the latter part of the 19th century. When tornadoes or floods struck the Ohio River area, crews from miles away could respond by boarding trains to reach the

disaster scenes. When the Mississippi River flooded in 1937, Coast Guard crews from all over the northeast responded to help their overburdened comrades already in that area. Lifeboat men moved from rooftop to rooftop, transporting the injured and sick to medical care, evacuating families from destroyed homes, and bringing food and other supplies to those people who could stay where they were. This gathering prepares to depart for the disaster zone.

The 36-foot-long motor lifeboat is now a thing of the past, but for the larger part of the 20th century, it was the primary search-and-rescue tool of the Coast Guard. Durable and tough, the boat could provide quite a ride for someone unfortunate enough to end up in the forward compartment after a rescue; it bounced on the waves enough to make a victim long for a return to his stricken vessel. The Coast Guard's most heroic rescue, by the service's own admission, took place on February 19, 1952, off Chatham, Cape Cod, Massachusetts, when coxswain Bernie Webber and his crew rescued more than 30 men from the sinking T-2 tanker *Pendleton* during a horrific storm. The crew of this boat off the New Jersey coast knows that, with an open cockpit, slick gear is needed to ensure as comfortable a ride as possible.

In this photograph taken off Barnegat, a Coast Guard crew in a 36-foot-long Class E motor lifeboat heads out for a drill. The Class E boats were preceded by 34-foot motor lifeboats, which were pulling boats fitted with engines. Again, a moment in time can be diagnosed. Note that the coastguardsmen wear cork life vests over their clothing, a staple of the old Life-Saving Service. As displayed here, the lifeboat could be fitted with sails and masts if needed in times of engine failure.

Lifeboat coxswains had to become experts in handling their boats in close quarters, especially near known shoals and ledges and along breakwaters. Here, a coxswain and a single crewman are either practicing or performing a rescue in Manasquan Inlet in their 36-foot-long Class T motor lifeboat (the third and final incarnation of the lifeboats of that length), just feet away from a breakwater that could potentially poke a hole in their boat. The Coast Guard has gone through two more generations of motor lifeboats since the 36-footer came into service. The 44-foot-long motor lifeboat began replacing the 36-footers in 1963, and the 47-footers began phasing out the 44-footers in the late 1990s.

Nothing could beat spending a day on the water the old-fashioned way, with or without a shirt on. Into the 1930s, crews from rival stations competed in rowing races and other contests, which provided a way for crews to maintain their skills while enjoying themselves at the same time. Close examination of the stress on the oars, not to mention the wake being thrown, shows just how seriously these men took their rowing. Alas, today it is one of the skills of the old Life-Saving Service that is all but disappearing in the service. With its many added missions, especially since its switch from the Department of Transportation to the new Department of Homeland Security, the already stretched-thin Coast Guard has enough to do to serve the public instead of searching for ways to keep tradition alive.

Despite all its public relations problems during the 1920s and 1930s, the Coast Guard came through Prohibition as strong as it had ever been. The service had experienced significant obstacles to its growth over the first two decades after its merger with the Revenue Cutter Service in 1915. In 1917, just two years after its formation and while still trying to find its new identity, the service was called to fall under the Department of the Navy for service in World War I. Then, shortly after the war ended, it took up the challenge of the war on rum. The shoreside servicemen went from lifesavers to warriors to federal law enforcement agents in the course of five years. In the years that followed, through World War II and beyond, they also became environmental and port-security specialists. Yet through it all, with public opinion on their side or not, the men (and now women) of the Coast Guard have always been ready to respond when storm warning flags go up, calling them to save the lives of mariners in distress on the sea.

Nine
ABOUT THE COLLECTION
EUGENE TOPPING OSBORN

Eugene Topping Osborn came from a long line of Osborns, the first of whom settled in this country in East Hampton, Long Island, New York. Many of his forefathers were seafaring men from Long Island's south shore. Capt. E. D. Topping, the great-grandfather of Eugene, was the first keeper of the 1849 lifesaving station at Moriches, Long Island. Eugene Topping Osborn was born on March 16, 1889, in East Moriches, Long Island. He grew up on the bay, boating, racing sailboats, clamming, and doing all the things young boys do around salt water. In 1913, at age 24, Eugene Topping Osborn joined the United States Life-Saving Service and was stationed at the surf station at Bellport, Long Island.

Osborn married Eva Hulse, and in 1917, as America prepared to enter World War I, Eva gave birth to a daughter, Barbara. Surfman Osborn fixed up a shack on the beach near the station and moved the family there during the winter of 1918 in hopes of escaping the terrible flu epidemic that was sweeping the nation. In 1915, the Life-Saving Service had merged with the Revenue Cutter Service to become the U.S. Coast Guard. Not much changed for the surfmen except that, for the first time in the history of the service, there were significant opportunities for advancement. Eugene, tutored by his schoolteacher wife, soon moved up the service's ladder.

Eugene Topping Osborn did what few managed to do: move up through the officer ranks without attending the Coast Guard Academy. He was commissioned ensign in 1925. The passage of the Volstead Act, the enforcement tool for the national prohibition of alcohol, found him in charge of the surf stations in New Jersey. The photographs in this book were taken for him at that time. He later returned to Long Island as the lieutenant in charge of the Fourth Coast Guard District, with headquarters in Bay Shore. In 1942, with the onset of World War II, the Coast Guard aligned its districts with the navy's districts, and the Long Island area became the Third Coast Guard District.

The hurricane of 1938 destroyed three Long Island Coast Guard stations, one of which was near the Moriches Inlet in East Moriches. Because of the danger the inlet posed to boaters, Moriches was rebuilt under the command of Eugene Topping Osborn, now a captain. He continued to be in charge of the Long Island area until his retirement in 1946. He built a retirement home on the bay he loved, and his daughter and her husband still live there. Captain Osborn died on March 19, 1957.

Ten
PRESERVING AMERICA'S LIFESAVING STATIONS

America's historic lifesaving stations today have many enemies—politicians, developers, and even Mother Nature among them. In recent years, buildings have fallen apart due to neglect, have been wiped clean out of existence by hurricanes, and have been prepared for demolition by city fathers who believe they can gain more revenue out of a duplex home than a historic lifesaving station. Yet, in almost every community, voices cry out in favor of preservation of these disappearing, sometimes unique, architectural structures. The Kiwanis Club of Cape May now inhabits the old Bibb No. 2–type Cold Spring Life-Saving Station.

Around the United States, many old stations are now proudly serving out their retirement as private homes, like the Rehoboth Beach, Delaware, station. Several stations serve as museums, city offices, or homes to other nonprofit organizations. Outwardly, they may not tell a story to the uninformed, but if their walls could talk, they would amaze passersby with tales of shipwrecks, heroism, tragedy, and the triumph of human will against unbeatable odds. Some might even have a story or two about the rumrunning era and the whispered rumors of what really happened in those days when the press was not paying attention.

The Lewes, Delaware, Life-Saving Station now shares a museum complex with the Overfalls Lightship, dutifully interpreting yet another facet of the Coast Guard life of the past. Dedicated volunteers go as far as polishing the brass of Lyle guns and Fresnel lighthouse lenses to keep their museums looking good.

Some stations have made it to the very brink of disaster before being pulled back. The station at Indian River, Delaware, now one of the country's finest lifesaving museums, was saved by a major restoration effort.

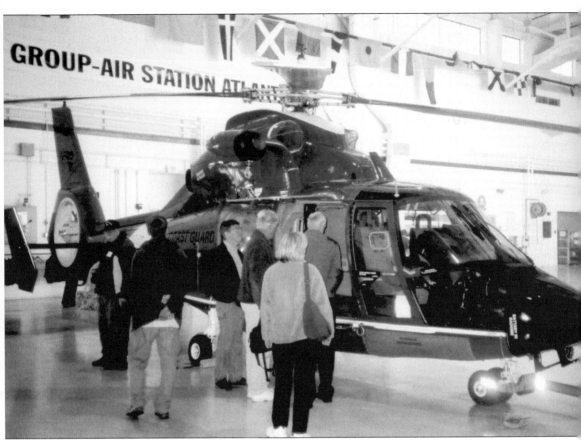

There can be no denying that the world of Coast Guard search-and-rescue operations has changed, and for the better, over the course of time. Lyle guns and breeches buoys have given way to HH-60 and HH-65 helicopters and other high-tech equipment, and pulling surf boats have faded out in favor of bigger, faster, and more capable lifeboats. But this does not mean that the heroes of the past, the boats they rowed, and the stations they lived and worked in should be forgotten.

Lifesaving stations like the old Ocean City, Maryland, building, now a very popular museum overlooking Assateague Inlet, can retell the tales of yore for all, including young Coast Guard men and women curious about the service's past.

In some instances, old Coast Guard stations—like this one at North Wildwood, New Jersey, which stands just in front of the Hereford Inlet Lighthouse—serve the public in other ways. The buildings have been put to use as offices of the National Marine Fisheries Service, field offices of the National Oceanic and Atmospheric Administration National Marine Sanctuary, or marine police barracks (exemplified by North Wildwood).

Notice Of Proposed Demolition

Take notice that the owner of this property intends to demolish the buildings and structures on this property pursuant to Ocean City, New Jersey Municipal Ordinance Number 25-1800.10.1.

Any person or organization interested in purchasing this property for its fair market value with the assurance that it will preserve the buildings and structures on the land please contact:

Steven D. Scherzer, Esquire

Cooper, Perskie, April, Niedelman, Wagenheim & Levenson, PA

1125 Atlantic Avenue · Third Floor
Atlantic City, NJ 08401 · (609) 572-7534

Not every remaining lifesaving station will stand forever, but the few that are left deserve a fighting chance to remind our nation of a long-forgotten service (the Life-Saving Service) and its often overlooked descendant (the Coast Guard).

Thanks to local, grass-roots organizations like the Save Our Station Coalition of Ocean City, New Jersey, and the national efforts of groups like the United States Life-Saving Service Heritage Association, not every station has to fall, and not all history has to be lost.